GOD'S ROADMAP

Mentally Releasing Stress & Pressure

Ronald R. Peterson II Ph.D.

GOD'S ROADMAP

For Information: 1891-3 Capital Circle NE # 104 Tallahassee, Florida
32308 Website: http://www.futureed4u.org

Printed in the United States of America

Peterson, Ron.
God's Roadmap: Mentally Releasing Stress & Pressure/ Ronald R.
Peterson II Ph.D. Includes bibliographical references and index.

ISBN-13: 978-1463728748
ISBN-10: 1463728743

1. Counseling 2. Biblical Studies 3. Stress

Editor: Cheryl Y. Peterson

Foreword

There are so many problems that are rooted in our stress and anxiety. This book from Ron Peterson will help you target the problems that result from stress, but more importantly present solutions that will be relevant to you. I have enjoyed getting to know and serve with Ron here in Midway. He uses his talents as Associate Pastor and Discipleship Pastor to help others grow in their faith. Ron, along with his beautiful wife Cheryl, serves faithfully at Fellowship. As you read this book, know that you are reading from a doctrinally stable and faithful man that loves the Lord! Blessings!

Doug Stephens

Senior Pastor

Fellowship @ Midway Church

Preface:

Pressure is something that strongly needs to be investigated from a Christian perspective. Many people are not quite sure what pressure is and/or how it happens. The formula for pressure is force over area as an organism's response to its environment. Pressure was originally studied in the 1950's. However, there is not much research on pressure and the spiritual aspects of it relating to the human body. Pressure can be externally measured by changes in skin reaction, gland secretions, and other physical ways. However, what about internal measurements? Pressure could cause un-do stress on the mind, the body, and the soul.

In this book, we will explore my theory of how applying Christian principles: such as, prayer, meditation, exaltation and praising of God, creates a weapon of defense that makes dealing with stress and pressure not just manageable for the mind, body and soul; but makes dealing with stress and press, on any level, a non-issue.

The breakdown to my research will start with the first level – the mental or 'the Mind'. From biblical understanding, the battle is fought in our mind. This is where we need to be guided and instructed from GOD on how to deal with everyday pressures. Since the fullness of my research will be very lengthy, I am focusing only on the mind for the first part of my research. The second level is physical or 'the Body'. Pressures can take a physical toll on the body. People's health is severely affected by the hardships of stress and pressure. GOD has a word for us in dealing with hardships of the world. There have been people who have mastered the art of living a stress-free life. However, no one truly lives stress free, but they have a peaceful life because of GOD. Those individuals have tapped into their true stress reliever – JESUS CHRIST. Focusing on the body will outline part two of the book series. The third and final level that I will be addressing is spiritual or 'the Soul'. "We fight not against flesh and blood but against principalities…" We must realize that the world is a spiritual realm and it uses stressful situations to help enslave us to this world. We must learn how to exercise God's Word in our everyday lives in order to overcome pressures and temptations. Research on the spiritual will be the final research in this series.

There are some major misconceptions that Christians only experience pressure if they are sinning or not doing the will of God. Christians usually experience pressure when they do not trust GOD.

Dealing with pressure effects us physically, mentally, and emotionally; pressure also disturbs the body's natural balance as well. Dealing with pressure cannot be avoided. It is a part of life. Some pressure could be good if we handle it in the proper way, but it could be detrimental and serious if we do not watch it.

There are many things that could be done mentally to relieve the stress one is experiencing from pressure. In this book, we will look at some ways to improve the quality of health of highly stressful people – Christians. The fellow believer is constantly under attack and must make sound and intelligent decisions every single day. However, we are called to cast our burdens on CHRIST because His Yoke is Easy.

Acknowledgements:

To GOD Be the Glory! Thank you LORD JESUS for strengthen me and giving me the insight to write the book and to help minister to other people. My Heavenly Father, I cannot thank you enough for the constant blessings, the constant forgiveness, the constant second chances, and for your constant grace in my life. My life truly has no purpose without you!

Next, to my beautiful wife Cheryl, thank you for all of your patience and support. I know it was not easy; I love you and I owe you so much. You have been incredibly strong throughout this whole process.

To my mother Linda, I could not have asked for a better mother than you. Thank you for always being there for me. To the rest of my family and the Peterson clan, I thank you all. All of you mean the world to me. All that I am today is a direct link and reflection of a beautiful family.

A special thanks to Dr. Johnson for your godly wisdom and insightful assistance; you especially helped me gather my thoughts to help shape this book. May the LORD continue to bless you and yours!

Thank you, to Pastor Stanley L. Walker and the church family of Tabernacle Missionary Baptist Church, located in Tallahassee, Florida. All of you fed me spiritual food when I departed from my home in Jacksonville, Fl. Thank you Tabernacle for the spiritual food that helps to sustain me.

To my church home: Fellowship @ Midway Church. A special thanks to my Pastor Doug L. Stephens. Thank you for seeing the JESUS that is in me, and for allowing me to be a part of your pastoral staff. As the rookie of the group, you guys (Doug, Bryan, and Tony) have set a hard act to follow: so let us continue to strive for excellence in doing Kingdom work. Thanks Doug Stephens, Bryan Mooneyhan, and Tony Tolson. A large part of my ministry of discipleship is being allowed to grow under the supervision of first, the Holy Spirit and secondly, from the leadership of Fellowship @ Midway Church here in Midway, FL.

I am so thankful and blessed to be able to preach and teach God's WORD. Thank you Fellowship of Midway Church for the opportunity to serve and be able to preach and teach God's WORD. .

Lastly, as the ole saying goes, "There's no place like home". To my first and beloved pastor: Pastor Rhim and my St. Joseph Missionary Baptist Church family. Pastor Rhim & Pastor Gregory, the 'prodigal son' comes back home in spirit to say, "Thank you for teaching me the WORD of GOD." My foundation is strong and sealed with the blood of JESUS CHRIST. From my parents (Ron & Linda), I have been turned over to the Church that started with St. Joseph. I am so thankful for all of you who have helped me become the Man of GOD that I am today.

Getting Started:

The Problem

Pressure! Millions of people all over the world try to deal with pressure without the aid of GOD. The problem is that millions of people are becoming sick due to stress and pressure in their everyday lives. Millions of people are concerned about their well-being and everyday quality of life. Many doctors, preachers, and life coaches all agree that stress and pressure is bad for the human body's physical, mental, and spiritual well-being. The countless number of stress related cases the health physician, preachers, and life coaches' deal with is increasing. Society in itself is starting to acknowledge that dealing with stress and pressure is a major concern in today's world. This research on dealing with pressure from a Christian's perspective is very important to acknowledge GOD in stressful times. GOD is the only true answer to combat life's pressure. People need to be made aware that there are benefits to Christian living.

"It is now clear, however, that psychological stress, particularly if chronic, can have deleterious effects on the body..." (Vander, Sherman, and Luciano, 2001 pg. 731). If prolonged and repeated, pressure could cause the sympathetic nervous system to activate which leads to high blood pressure. The increased cortisol associated with stress "can decrease the activity of the immune system enough to reduce the body's resistance to infection" and can "worsen the symptoms of diabetes because of its anti-insulin effects, and it can cause increased rate of death of neurons." (Vander, Sherman, and Luciano, 2001, pg. 731). After awhile, the body dealing with pressure causes the body to shut down. The shutting down of the body leaves us exposed to harmful symptoms that could go un-notice if we are not checked out.

The digestive system and other internal organs are slowed down so the majority of the blood flow can be directed to the muscles. The problem with this is pressure over time could lead to chronic illness. Long periods of stress and pressure interfere with the way the body functions. Then you begin to notice physical symptoms, which are a warning sign that stress and pressure is over-taking the body.

As continued research is reviewed, we see that pressure can affect our health unexpectedly. Dealing with pressure could be continuing headaches, loss of concentration, and a poor work ethic. Stress and pressure affects all parts of the body from the mental to the spiritual.

Further research states, "The human body is designed to experience stress and react to it. Stress can be positive, keeping us alert and ready to avoid danger. Stress becomes negative when a person faces continuous challenges without relief or relaxation between challenges. As a result, the person becomes overworked and stress-related tension builds.

Stress that continues without relief can lead to a condition called distress -- a negative stress reaction. Distress can lead to physical symptoms including headaches, upset stomach, elevated blood pressure, chest pain, and problems sleeping. Research suggests that stress also can bring on or worsen certain symptoms or diseases.

Stress also becomes harmful when people use alcohol, tobacco, or drugs to try to relieve their stress. Unfortunately, instead of relieving the stress and returning the body to a relaxed state, these substances tend to keep the body in a stressed state and cause more problems.

Consider the following:

• Forty-three percent of all adults suffer adverse health effects from stress.
• Seventy-five percent to 90% of all doctor's office visits are for stress-related ailments and complaints.
• Stress can play a part in problems such as headaches, high blood pressure, heart problems, diabetes, skin conditions, asthma, arthritis, depression, and anxiety.
• The Occupational Safety and Health Administration (OSHA) declared stress a hazard of the workplace. Stress costs American industry more than $300 billion annually.
• The lifetime prevalence of an emotional disorder is more than 50%, often due to chronic, untreated stress reactions" (Kieffer)

"Stress is one of the things of life that seems difficult to avoid. With hectic schedules associated with school, work, and family; so much to do, things that do not go as planned, conflicts, and losses of various kinds, etc., the weight of pressure rises. The key is in learning how to manage in spite of it all. I do not believe there is any one of us that does not have some sort of stress to deal with from time to time. We each deal with varying stresses in different ways and looking around us we see some who seem to deal with it all pretty well, while others do not. However, it is not always so much the object of the stress as much as it is the length of time it is being endured that creates the greatest weight upon us" (Hanson, 2007).

Review of the Research

We must deal with the actions of stress and pressure on the body. The research collected will show the seriousness of stress and pressure on the body, and the decrease of affects that stress has on the body when you rely on JESUS CHRIST.

However, in this research we will look at the differences of stress in the Average Person from the Active Christian who deals with the same type of stress but differently. There are unique differences between the average person's stress and pressure tolerance level and that of a fellow Active Christian. We will focus on what Active Christians do differently from the Average Person and how those differences affect the body.

There is not much research devoted to dealing with stress and pressure from a Christian's perspective. Therefore, a survey was performed to give an in-depth working knowledge of how relying on Christians practices (mostly prayer and meditation), depending on JESUS CHRIST would significantly reduce your stress and pressure level. This study compares active Christians to average people in their levels of stress and pressure in their lives and how they handle it. This research will be one of the foundations of looking at stress and pressure on people and comparing that to the presence of GOD in their lives. These results are based on a small sample of people and more research is needed.

Implications of the Research

The theoretical framework for this research is based on CHRIST and the theory of prayer and obedience to GOD will reduce your stress and pressure and make light your burdens. Believing in the power of GOD and practicing faith in your everyday life will make living less in vain than others who may not be practicing this lifestyle. This research will use Christian people and compare them with the Average Person who may or may not be an active practicing Christian. This survey will give us insight into people's stress and pressure levels, and examine ways they practice dealing with stress and pressure. Also, this survey will reveal methods of Christians in how they deal with stress and pressure, therefore, providing data that will be used to develop a basis on dealing with all types of stress and pressure. One goal of this research is to open the eyes of the people who may not have accepted CHRIST as LORD and SAVIOR. In addition, I hope to inspire the Christians who are not active and/or not living according to the WORD of GOD.

Most Christians believe that when stress and pressure hit, that is an opportunity to get closer with GOD; along with some practical ways that Christians should do is outlined in the WORD of GOD. Getting enough rest is critical; there are many directives given in the bible on just rest itself. Christians should have a proper diet where they are getting the necessary nutrients that are needed from healthy foods. Regular exercise is also mentioned in Scripture. But in my opinion, the most important of all is a healthy balance between work and church. Personal family time with the family is critical. The family is our daily support system; especially when all else fails. GOD gives us a family so we can get a taste of God's family unit. These are some practical ways suggested by the Bible that relates to stress and pressure. The benefit of Christian living is unmeasured. My hope is to expand the minds of all individuals to see the benefits of JESUS CHRIST as LORD of your life.

The power of prayer is undefined and cannot be measured. God's grace and mercy is without limit and is big and vast that mere men cannot comprehend. The Bible suggests, "Take EVERYTHING to GOD in prayer." GOD is the X Factor that can make an impossible thing possible. Christians believe this as a basic truth, and therefore, a lot of stress and pressure is avoided. So with all of this said, my belief is to open the door for all to see the power of JESUS CHRIST. I want to spark the interest in all to seek JESUS no matter what they are going through. Meditation on God's WORD is essential for dealing with stress and pressure. GOD has given us countless blessings and promises that are outlined in HIS WORD. We just have to remember those promises and keep reciting them in our spirit. Especially in times of trouble, GOD is forever faithful and will not abandon us or HIS promises for our lives. GOD loves us no matter if we love Him or not. GOD sent His Son JESUS CHRIST to die for all of our sins.

Lastly, we are to Worship the LORD at all times. When we are doing well and when we are doing badly, GOD is still worthy of our praises. Just by GOD giving us life in itself, HE is worthy in being praised. GOD has given us the gift of salvation and if He did not do anything else, that alone is a reason to worship the LORD. We must remember this at all time. To GOD be the Glory!

The Purpose of the Study

This research will inform and reconfirm the benefits of relying on JESUS CHRIST for stress and pressure relief and de-escalating pressure in your everyday life. There will be a few questions that will be targeted in this research. One, is there a benefit in relying on JESUS to handle our problems versus not relying on Him? Another question to consider; is there a difference between the Average person's stress and pressure level versus an Active Christian's stress and pressure level? I want to focus on the differences in terms of percentages to see if the differences are minimal or significant.

Another purpose of this study is to review Christian principles' in reducing stress and pressures in their everyday life. The principles that are outlined could be used in any environment such as work, home, church, and in other social events. People have to be taught how to survive, or where to go and seek help. My desire is to do both, show the benefits of Christian living, and tell everyone about JESUS CHRIST. JESUS is who you turn to when things are going good to praise Him, and JESUS is who you turn to when things are going bad to worship Him. Then people would know how to cover themselves under all circumstances.

This research is design to solve the problem of how to deal with stress and pressure from a Christian perspective. This research will reveal a blue print in reducing the pressure in your life with Christian principles. Like with anything the 'Road Map' was giving to us by GOD. It is contained in His Holy Book - the Bible. I am merely opening up God's Word for all of us to see and read. As the old saying goes, "You can lead a horse to water but you cannot make him drink." My hope is that all will exercise our free will and partake in the 'Living Water' JESUS has for all of us. This research will inform fellow Christians of the benefits of having CHRIST as our personal LORD and SAVIOR. This research will also give us a glimpse of the harshness of the outside world, and how it can affect us mentally, spiritually, and physically without CHRIST in your life. There are many examples of the harsh effect to stress and pressure on the human body. People are dying at alarming rates due to stress and pressure. Even with all of the advance medicines we have today, there is no substitute for JESUS CHRIST in our lives. He alone can make an unhealthy situation healthy and vibrant.

Research Questions & Design

Are there affects on the mental, spiritual, and physical aspect of the human body when one relies on JESUS CHRIST as their personal LORD and SAVIOR versus the Average Person who may or may not be an Active Christian? What are the things Christian people do that are different from the Average Person when dealing with stress and pressure? Are there benefits to having JESUS CHRIST as a personal LORD and SAVIOR? How much affect is the presence of GOD in Active Christians lives different from the Average Person who may or may not live accordingly to the WORD of GOD? There will be a survey conducted of 100 people; 50 of them will be Active Christians and 50 will be Average People who may or may not be an Active Christian.

My hypothesis:

I believe that there will be a tremendous decrease in stress and pressure for active Christians using principles that GOD outlined in His Word. I believe the GOD factor in Active Christian lives will reduce the harmful effects of stress and pressure versus the Average Person.

Method:

The method of this research is to conduct a survey of Active Christians and the Average Person will be the basis of this research. There will be twenty questions asked of 100 people chosen. There were 50 Active Christians and 50 Average people targeted for this research. I will focus on three different dimension of stress: the mental, the physical, and the spiritual. The data would be collected and analyzed for the GOD factor in people's lives.

Now we are in the car of life ready to take off, but where are we going? In chapter one, we will look at God's Map to see where our destination lies. God's Map is clearly laid out for us to read; we just need to pick it up (Holy Bible), and start reading it. God's full plan is fully revealed for us to follow.

Table of Contents

Chapter 1: Reading the Map

Before we can literally and figuratively get in the car and drive off to destinations unknown, we need to look at the map to see where we have been, where we are, and where we are going. If we look at this from a spiritual and mental point of view, then we would start with the Holy Bible, God's Roadmap for our lives. What is God's plan for our lives? Well, in His WORD lies the Roadmap. It is right in front of us and not hidden from our view.

In the Beginning, GOD created the world and put man in it. The WORD of GOD says that GOD formed man *of* the dust of the ground, and breathed into his nostrils the breath of life; and man became a living being. (Gen 2:7). Therefore, this is the first destination on God's Roadmap, Man came from GOD. That is the where. However, why was man formed? The WORD of GOD tells us that in the beginning, GOD created the Heavens and the Earth, day and night, and all the animals on the planet. His culminating creation was Man:

Man was made last of all creatures. He could take no honor to himself as contributing toward the work of creation. And as the last of God's creative work he was honored and appointed ruler of the entire creation. (Bible Beliefs, p.15)

Then GOD said, *"Let Us make man in Our image, according to Our likeness; let them have dominion over the fish of the sea, over the birds of the air, and over the cattle, over all the Earth and over every creeping thing that creeps on the Earth."* (Genesis 1:26)

Subsequently, man understood his identity; He was a Son of GOD made in the image of his father GOD in Heaven. Last of all, the creatures were manmade. No glory for himself could Man take in creation. GOD crowned man ruler of the universe. Dust of the ground was man formed, the materials, which makes up man, confirms modern science reveals all the elements come from the Earth.

GOD'S ROADMAP:

After the body was formed, then GOD breathed in man's nostrils and he became a living soul. So man was made like his creator, in his image. And once man ceases from existence his body goes back into the ground and his soul goes back to GOD who gave it. (Eccles. 12:7).

As we journey through God's map people often form certain questions in their minds: Who am I? Where is my position in life? What is my purpose in this world? Is there any significance in my life? Each one of these questions is a point on God's Roadmap. We must fully understand who we are and how we became to be in order to know where we are going. People often want fulfillment and satisfaction in life and they usually turn to other factors to find it, instead of GOD, who is the only one that can fulfill every person's needs. Do not look for an outer solution where it is found inwardly.

In the beginning, Adam was in the full glory of GOD before sin entered into the world. Adam walked with his Father, GOD in the garden (identity). Adam had dominion over all the land (position) and Adam was commanded by GOD to be fruitful and multiply which gave him (purpose). There was great meaning to Adam to praise and please GOD (significance). Adam experienced fulfillment in every way from and with GOD. Adam's fall broke the relationship of fulfillment he was experiencing with GOD. To get that longing feeling of completeness back, man has to be in constant fellowship with GOD through prayer & worship. Man will constantly thirst to have all of his needs met, the spirit of GOD that was placed in man longs to be with Him. So it is a constant struggle that could wheel tremendous stress in all people.

Identity, position, purpose, and significance (IPPS) are family concepts realized through the institution of family. _As children grow up, they look for answers to these questions and for an avenue to satisfy these needs. Within the family system, these concepts become functional. Children discover who they are as individuals in relationship to the family (identify). They learn through the family system where they fit in and belong (position). They gain a reason for being and find (purpose) in family duties. Children feel appreciated and know the value of their contribution to the family (significance)._

2

The family system as GOD designed it, establishes an avenue where these needs are first met and prepares children to transition to and become functional members of His larger family- the Kingdom of GOD.

Children brought up in a loving, godly environment become responsible, healthy adults prepared for Kingdom work, who easily embrace their identity, position, purpose, and significance within God's family and Kingdom. (Christian Counseling, p.83)

It is so important to understand the (IPPS) when reading God's roadmap. Our identity is found in JESUS. We are children of the Most High GOD. We have promises and blessings that our father in Heaven has granted to us. Take advantage of accepting JESUS CHRIST as our personal LORD and SAVIOR. A deeper look into family gives us insight to characteristics of GOD. GOD permitted a father, a mother, and children to be the makeup of a traditional family. God's family consist of GOD the Father, GOD the Son, GOD the Holy Spirit, and us the children of GOD. We are part of God's family and we were designed for that purpose.

Our position is found in JESUS. Spiritually we are in the driver seat while CHRIST is in the passenger seat. GOD has given us dominion over the Earth and all that is in it. Our destination is Heaven in JESUS CHRIST. We can connect to GOD at anytime using our GPS JESUS CHRIST. We can overcome wrong turns by getting back on the right street JESUS. We have to remember we are the head and not the tail. As a child of GOD, our position is secured and we should never be beaten down with stress and pressure.

Our purpose is found in JESUS. GOD has a special roadmap just for us. The only thing we have to do is just follow Him. We have been designed from the beginning to be fruitful and multiply. We are the hands and feet of CHRIST. We need to go out and work His ministry. At times we allow stress and pressure to handicap us and not do what we are called to do, which is go out and share the 'Good News' of JESUS CHRIST. Keep in mind that things may be going crazy because we are not walking in our purpose.

Our significance is found in JESUS. The reason why we exist is for the glory of GOD. As we go through out this journey, we are to stop at rest stops and share the good news of

JESUS CHRIST. That is significant because the more we tell others, then they can share the Good News with others and it spreads all over the world. Therefore, our efforts in sharing JESUS are never in vain and we will be rewarded in heaven for our faithfulness. Therefore, our life has a new meaning when we accept JESUS CHRIST as our personal LORD and SAVIOR. We are not living for our self anymore we have another higher factor in which we serve to the fullest of the Glory and Honor of GOD.

It is so important to understand where we were and how we got to this point in life before we can continue on our journey of life. GOD has laid out the map to follow and at times, we mess up the directions by NOT obeying all the signs and signals GOD leaves for us to navigate our way through. When we make a wrong turn we need to do a U-turn as quick as possible, but there are times that a u-turn is NOT possible. We may find ourselves on a one-way street, when we get to that point, then we need to keep going until we find the right way on the map. That street is called JESUS CHRIST. JESUS says, *"I am the way and the truth and the life. No one comes to the Father except through me."* (John 14:6) Man had lost his way since the beginning, with Adam and Eve in the Garden of Eden. We needed to be reconciled back to GOD and there was none righteous in the eyes of GOD who could fulfill this requirement. The bible says, *"As it is written, there is none righteous, no not one: There is none that understands, there is none that seeks after GOD. They all gone out of the way, they are together become unprofitable, there is none that does good, no not one."* (Romans 3:10-12)

Now, one might wonder if we must be righteous and there is no one on the Earth that fits that description, then how can one be saved. The answer to that question is found with and in JESUS CHRIST. JESUS said, "With man it is impossible, but with GOD all things are possible." In other words, no man can be saved except through JESUS

CHRIST. JESUS is the only way to be redeemed, and when stressful times come, active Christians grab hold to this fact.

Therefore, as long as one drives on the road of Righteousness, he or she has life abiding in him or her, but if he or she wanders off the road of righteousness, then they are on a one-way street that leads to death.

Moreover, the only street that leads to GOD is driving on and towards JESUS CHRIST. Once again, we must not be knocked off from our path of JESUS when trials, problems, and hardships arise. These circumstances are all forms of stress and pressure. Remember, do not lose focus, and keep your eyes on JESUS.

Man understood his purpose to have dominion over everything in the universe. Man is God's ambassador or representative. Man is constantly tapping into the knowledge of Science to help shape and mold the natural world. This ordains man's authority over nature. GOD also gave man responsibility for what he was governing. GOD gave commands for man to follow, and out of love, man did what was according to God's Will until a certain point. At that point, sin entered into the world along with stress and pressure of the world.

While man was driving alone, GOD saw fit to give man a co-pilot to ride with him. GOD said, "It is not good that man should be alone; I will make him a helper comparable to him." (Genesis 2:18) Woman and man are to complement one another. The two together make up one body one flesh. Matthew Henry wrote, "The woman was formed out of man, not out of his head to rule over him, not out of his feet to be a doormat, but out of his side to be his equal." Now man has his co-pilot and they are ready for the road of life.

However, while man (Adam) and woman (Eve) was driving. They made a pit stop and got off the main road (GOD). While man was busy, he left his woman exposed to an attack from the Devil. Instead of following God's Roadmap for their lives, mankind thought they could drive the car without God's supervision or guidance. The Devil picked on the weaker vessel – woman. However, it was man's responsibility to look after her and in that regard, Man failed. The

Devil played on the intelligence of man by letting him think that he could provide his own roadmap that would be equal to God's roadmap, and that man was capable of providing his own way. Look at what the Devil says, "For GOD knows that in the day you eat of it your eyes will be opened, and you will be like GOD knowing good and evil." (Genesis 3:5) So even with woman and man off the road GOD still had a plan for them.

GOD issued judgment on them; however, God's Roadmap was still revealed to them in his WORD. GOD said, "And I will put enmity between you and the woman, and between your seed and her Seed; He shall bruise your head, and you shall bruise His heel." (Genesis 3:15) GOD reveal that CHRIST would come through woman and provide the final piece for our reconciliation back to Him. This is God's Roadmap revealed; the only thing for us to do is to accept His Son JESUS CHRIST as our personal LORD and SAVIOR.

With the introduction of sin, husband and wife now experience conflict; which can take a toll on us mentally, physically, and spiritually. This is another form of stress and pressure. There are some helpful ways in dealing with stress and pressure in a marriage. Number one, communicate. No one should ever break the line of communication. When there is a problem between a husband and a wife, they should always talk about the situation. There is no such thing about not talking about a situation in order to avoid arguing about it. The situation will resurface at some point in time. As for arguing - it is healthy in a relationship; it is a form of communication. We just have to remember to argue fairly and not try to hurt one another in the process. GOD said it best, "A house divided cannot stand." Remember that a husband and a wife is one. Two bodies come together and make one; one body and one soul that make up a marriage. Number two, always use love in your marriage. Actually, it could be number one because if you love your spouse you would communicate with him or her even in conflict. Love them with your words, love them with your whole heart, and love them with your entire mind. Lastly, always be willing to compromise. No one can win them all. We are not design to win all the time in life because we experience trials and tribulations. Therefore, with that said, then we should not want to win every argument, every fight, or every disagreement. We must be willing to die to our flesh and selfish desires in order to be in a position to compromise and deny self.

Understanding ourselves is critical before we take off. Do we really know ourselves? What do we really see when we look in the car mirror? Chapter 2 gives us deeper insight into ourselves. Are we ready to understand ourselves?

Renewing our Purpose:

Upon the completion of this chapter, we should know: that GOD has a plan for our lives. If we are concerned and/or worried - if GOD loves us, then all we have to do is look at God's roadmap for our lives. It is found in God's WORD - the Holy Bible, and I have outlined it as well in Chapter 1.

Struggling with a Situation:

We are worried about world problems such as bills, sickness, and setbacks; one starts to wonder if GOD cares for us or cares if we are in a situation needing help. When this situation starts to occur, sometimes we lose hope and doubt God's WORD that He is with us and never will leave us.

Reading the Proclaim:

"But GOD, who is rich in mercy, for his great love wherewith he loved us, Even when we were dead in sins, hath quickened us together with CHRIST, (by grace ye are saved;) And hath raised us up together, and made us sit together in heavenly places in CHRIST JESUS: That in the ages to come he might show the exceeding riches of his grace in his kindness towards us through CHRIST JESUS." (Ephesians 2:4-7)

Making our Routine Permanent: As we meditate on this situation, let us be reminded:

That GOD is greater than your problems! Keep in mind that GOD cares and in Him should you place your trust. Remember, in order for GOD to be active in your life you first must turn over your life to Him. GOD cannot be GOD to you, until you let him. GOD has given you free will; however, you must learn to submit to His.

Conducting a Righteous Project:

Write down some experiences of times when you did not understand what GOD was doing, but now, as you look back on past events, after the fact, you now understand things clearly:

_____

_____

_____

_____

_____

_____

_____

_____

_____

Meditating on a Reflective Prayer:

LORD JESUS, give me the faith to trust YOU when things are not so clear, give me the comfort to know that you are close, and that you care for me. In Jesus' name, I pray. Amen.

Chapter 2: Staring Back in the Car Mirror

Often at times, before we start our journey, we look in the car mirror to see ourselves. However, what is it that we really see? "Throughout time, there have been four characteristics found in every person: a belief system, creative genius, conscience (knowing good and evil), and identity. Every part of man wants to connect back with GOD. GOD has put eternity in his or her hearts, except, no one can find out the work that GOD does from beginning to end (Ecclesiastes 3:11). This type of yearning for GOD by man causes him to search for GOD or something greater than himself. Nevertheless, as we learned in chapter one, that fulfillment only comes from GOD.

We must understand who we are and whose we are. When we are right with GOD, we reflect His image and His nature. Therefore, we bring constant glory and honor to GOD. This is a concept of living stress free; because, as long we are bringing glory and honor to GOD, we are constantly in the spirit and not in the flesh.

Taking a closer look in the car mirror we see nothing, because at times we lack a believe system; we have the spirit of fear, and will find ourselves in bad predicaments. When our ability to create is misguided, then we become lustful of things in the world. When we refuse to accept the rules for good and evil, we are full of self-pride. At that point, we decide to do our own will and not God's Will. When we fail to identify who we are and whom we belong to, we find ourselves in idolatry, worshipping everything that is not of GOD. This is when stress and pressure arises.

GOD first warned Adam in the Garden of Eden not to eat from the tree of good and evil or he will die. Adam did not die physically, but spiritually when he ate of the fruit. In addition, by Adam, every man enters the world with the sin nature; therefore, man is filled with emotions and feelings that differ from time to time. Because of this, man now experiences stress and pressure mentally, physically, and spiritually.

It is very important to understand ourselves. If we look at Abraham Maslow, he proposed a hierarchy of needs that represented many needs that motivate human behavior. At the very top of his hierarchy is self-actualization. Self-actualization is the desire for self-fulfillment. Once again, true fulfillment can ONLY be found in JESUS CHRIST.

Man exists in three parts created in the image of GOD. Man is a spirit with a soul living in a body. Each part connects with one another and is therefore affect by the others. However, the focus in this book will be the soul or 'the mind'.

Breakdown the soul: the soul of a man is made up of feelings, his mind, and his will power. We must recognize this before we can understand how man is made up.

Feelings:

The definition of feelings is a mental state that arises spontaneously rather than through conscious effort, and is often accompanied by physiological changes. It is how we feel at a given time and it varies from moment to moment. However, lean on the side of caution, when reacting out of feelings. Feelings and emotions could betray us from making a sound judgment or a decision at times.

The Mind:

The definition of the mind is the human consciousness that originates in the brain and is manifested especially in thought, perception, feelings, will, memory, and imagination. The mind is where the spiritual battle is fought. The mind houses your soul as well. A warning about the mind: do not be too logical to the point where you have an inability to feel. Remember, GOD gave us emotions and feelings; it is ok to use them.

Will Power:

The will is the mental faculty by which one deliberately chooses or decides upon a course of action. Will, is having self- discipline and/or will power.

It is very important to understand who we are, and what we are made up of. We can better communicate with our co-pilot (spouse) who is riding in the car of life with us. Communication is the key to having a successful relationship with our co-pilot. There would be fewer arguments and fewer distractions from taking our eyes off the road. The better we understand ourselves the more we can compromise when our co-pilot and we disagree while in motion.

Before we take off - we should have identified some goals that we want to accomplish; however, our number one goal should be a faithful, obedient child of GOD. Albert Bandura, believes in self-efficacy, which is a person's belief in his or her ability to succeed in certain situations. However, I believe this should be the case in all situations of life that we can rise above any challenging situation. I share the 'belief in self-efficacy that we should develop a deeper interest in activities we do, form a stronger sense of commitment, and recover quickly from setbacks and disappointments.' (Bandura, 1994)

Bandura wrote, "The most effective way of developing a strong sense of efficacy is through mastery experiences." (Bandura, 1994) We are thankful that GOD gives us plenty of opportunities to master everyday experiences called trials and tribulations. It is so important to follow others as they are following CHRIST. If we are traveling after other cars on the road leading to CHRIST, then we are on the right road. Bandura stated, "By learning how to minimize stress and elevate mood when facing difficult or challenging tasks, people can improve their sense of self-efficacy. (Bandura, 1992) This is the very bases for writing this book; I want to encourage fellow Christians to depend on the LORD for relief of life's pressures in their lives.

Numerous people are tearing themselves down, deep down hating on themselves. This must stop; a person who hates him or herself can- not love another. We can- not give someone what we do not have to give. We can- not love someone else when we hate ourselves. How can we build up when we are low? We cannot. 'Self-image is the most important thing in the world that we need to have next to our faith in GOD. It does not matter what others think of you. It matters only what you think of you based upon what GOD thinks of you.' (Jakes, 1997) Active Christians have an excellent idea of who they are through CHRIST JESUS.

The next step is overcoming your past, which often is a tall task, but in chapter, 3 lies the necessary information needed to get over tough trials and tribulations.

Renewing our Purpose:

Upon the completion of this chapter, we should know: that GOD has given everyone of us an identity. If we accept His Son JESUS CHRIST as LORD and SAVIOR, we could have a renowned sense of who we are. Lastly, we should dedicate our life in doing God's Will then we could experience true fulfillment.

Struggling with a Situation:

Are you depressed? Do you stay depress? Have you found yourself experiencing mood swings? Every time a new problem arises, you lose control of your emotions. Are you ready for a change?

Reading the Proclaim:

"Then said JESUS unto His disciples, If any man will come after me, let him deny himself, and take up his cross, and follow me. For whosoever will save, his life shall lose it: and whosoever will lose his life for my sake shall find it. For what is a man profited, if he shall gain the whole world, and lose his own soul? Or what shall a man give in exchange for his soul?" (Matthew 16:24-26)

Making our Routine Permanent: As we contemplate on this situation, let us be reminded:

That GOD created us in His image and in His likeness. We are powerful beyond measure. It is better for us to do self-denial (follow God's Will for our life) than Bandura's view of self-efficacy. Self-efficacy is good to strive for - just keep it in its proper perspective, under God's Will.

Conducting a Righteous Project:

Read the folktale of the carrot, the coffee bean, and the egg. Write down which one you are and why. Then pray that GOD gives you the strength to maintain or the strength to change.

'The Carrot, the Coffee Bean, and the Egg:'

A young woman went to her mother and told her about her life and how things were so hard for her. She did not know how she was going to make it and wanted to give up. She was tired of fighting and struggling. It seemed as one problem was solved, a new one arose.

Her mother took her to the kitchen. She filled three pots with water and placed each on a high fire. Soon the pots came to boil. In the first, she placed carrots, in the second, she placed eggs, and in the last, she placed ground coffee beans. She let them sit and boil, without saying a word. In about twenty minutes, she turned off the burners. She fished the carrots out and placed them in a bowl. She pulled the eggs out and placed them in a bowl. Then she ladled the coffee out and placed it in a bowl.

Turning to her daughter, she asked, "Tell me, what you see?" "Carrots, eggs, and coffee," she replied. Her mother brought her closer and asked her to feel the carrots. She did and noted that they were soft. The mother then asked the daughter to take an egg and break it. After pulling off the shell, she observed the hard-boiled egg. Finally, the mother asked the daughter to sip the coffee. The daughter smiled, as she tasted its rich aroma. The daughter then asked, "What does it mean, mother?" Her mother explained that each of these objects had faced the same adversity ... boiling water. Each reacted differently. The carrot went in strong, hard, and unrelenting. However, after being subjected to the boiling water, it softened and became weak. The egg had been fragile. Its thin outer shell had protected its liquid interior, but after sitting through the boiling water, its inside became hardened. The ground coffee beans were unique, however. After they were in the boiling water, they had changed the water.

"Which are you?" she asked her daughter. "When adversity knocks on your door, how do you respond? Are you a carrot, an egg, or a coffee bean?" Think of this: Which are you? Are you the carrot that seems strong, but with pain and adversity do you wilt, become soft, and lose your strength? Are you the egg that starts with a malleable heart, but changes with the heat? Do you have a fluid spirit, but after a death, a breakup, a financial hardship or some other trial? Do you become hardened and stiff? Does your shell look the same, but on the inside are you bitter and tough with a stiff spirit and hardened heart?

Or are you like the coffee bean? The bean actually changes the hot water, the very circumstance that brings the pain. When the water gets hot, it releases the fragrance and flavor. If you are like the bean, when things are at their worst, you get better and change the situation around you." When the hour is the darkest and trials are their greatest, do you elevate yourself to another level. How do you handle adversity? Are you a carrot, an egg, or a coffee bean? Why?

_____

_____

_____

The Carrot, the Coffee Bean, and the Egg, American Folktale author Anonymous

Meditating on a Reflective Prayer:

My FATHER, thank you for being my GOD and my SAVIOUR. Thank you for being my Shepherd in my time of need. In Christ's name I pray. Amen.

Chapter 3: Looking in the Rear View Mirror

We need to focus on the road ahead and NOT constantly on the road behind us. One of the biggest ways of getting into a car accident is taking our eyes off the road ahead. At times, we are constantly looking back thinking about what we just passed, and we think that the past can somehow catch us and do major damage. However, the real danger is the obstacles that are ahead of us and not behind us. We must let the past be the past. Yes, the past is a part of us, but we cannot and should not let the past consume us.

When we are unable to move forward, something or someone has a hold on us. One of the first things we should do is identify what has a hold on us and what is keeping us from moving forward. When we are trying to move forward but cannot, that tends to lead one to feel stressed and pressured. Whenever we are stuck, take it to GOD in prayer.

Are we stuck in park? We should be able to move forward but cannot. We put our foot to the pedal and step on the gas but still nothing. Are we tired of seeing the same sights in our lives? However, we cannot move forward. Are we ready to explore more streets? Nevertheless, we are stuck in park. GOD has the power to set us free through CHRIST JESUS.

"Stress turns into pressure, and pressure into rage, and constant rage creates a state of weariness. Webster defines weary, in part, as having 'your sense of pleasure exhausted.' When we are weary, nothing is exciting. Everything seems bland. We become numb, unable to act or even believe that change can come. Everyday seems like the day before." (Jakes, p.168)

The pressures of life affect us all. No one is exempt! The pressures of life can make us immobile, unable, or unwilling to drive the car in the right direction. We must become focus and we do this by aligning our minds in CHRIST JESUS. HE is our true navigational system. We are over comers to stress and pressure being children of GOD.

We may not be able to change the direction of our lives, but we can change the direction of the car. Remember, we control the steering wheel; all we have to do is follow the road that leads to JESUS. So do not wait any longer! GOD has given us the ability to do incredible things! Start by changing our condition today by turning to JESUS.

Life happens to everyone; however, we cannot allow our past to keep us in park. Life's problems should not keep us from getting pass our past. We need a change of scenery. Having a renewing of the spirit of GOD would be the change of pace we need. We can do this through revivals, retreats, workshops, and simply by visiting a bible teaching church where JESUS CHRIST is taught as LORD. This will build up our spirit, soul, and body. GOD rewards those who constantly seek Him. Whatever we stand in need of - go and take it to GOD. He hears all and knows all.

Having a positive self-esteem is critical in over-coming our past. We need to start with having a positive relationship with the LORD. Then, have a personal pep rally! We have to encourage ourselves even when there is no one around to encourage us.

The next chapter deals with anxiety. Dealing with anxiety is never fun - but necessary in dealing with life. We must master effective ways in dealing with it, and I have a few ways of dealing with anxiety that I want to share.

Renewing our Purpose:

Upon the completion of this chapter: we should know that we have the power and the capability to overcome our past. Our past is just shadows as we go forward in the light. Renew ourselves in the Spirit of GOD to conquer anything that we face. Do not allow our problems and situations to keep us from moving forward.

Struggling with a Situation:

Is your past constantly coming up? Are you tired of being distracted? Are you tired of taking your eyes off the road of life and constantly looking back? You cannot focus on the task at hand? Are you stuck? Do you have a feeling of emptiness?

Reading the Proclaim:

"I will lift up my eyes to the hills—
　　From whence comes my help?
My help *comes* from the LORD,
　　Who made heaven and earth.
The LORD shall preserve you from all evil;
　　He shall preserve your soul.
The LORD shall preserve your going out and your coming in
　　From this time forth, and even forevermore.

GOD in the ages to come he might shew the exceeding riches of his grace in his kindness towards us through CHRIST JESUS. " (Psalm 121:1-2 & 7-8)

Making our Routine Permanent: As we contemplate on this situation, let us be reminded:

GOD sits high and looks low. HE can guide you when you seem lost, when we seem stuck and cannot go forward. GOD knows all and is all - powerful. GOD also cares for us and wants the very best for us.

Conducting a Righteous Project:

Read this poem and write down all the people who are in your life now, and write down what they bring to your life. Think about the ones that use to be in your life and the things they brought to your life, good or bad. Now, how have you grown for the new people that are in your life now?

'There comes a point in your life when you realize:

who matters,

who never did,

who won't anymore...

and who always will.

So, don't worry about people from your past,

there's a reason why they didn't make it to your future.'

_____

_____

_____

_____

Meditating on a Reflective Prayer:

Thank you GOD for your guidance, you are the Good and Faithful Shepherd. I thank you for your grace and mercy. Heavenly Father, may you continue to order my steps in your WORD, in Jesus' name. Amen.

There is a Point in Your Life, American Poem author Anonymous.

Chapter 4: Spinning Out of Control

What do we do when we find ourselves spinning out of control? We are in the car of life and nothing we do seem to be working. The car will not stop spinning in order for us to make a decision on which direction to go. Our life is filled with anxiety on every level. Anxiety is a synonym for stress and pressure. Therefore, we must be knowledgeable on what we are dealing with when we are dealing with anxiety. Moreover, if we do not know what the anxiety really is, then go and seek God's guidance.

As I read the book Competent To Counsel, by Jay E. Adams, I realized that one of the first things we should do is confess our sins to GOD. Jay Adams believes 'God's remedy for man's problem is confession. The concealing of transgressions brings misery, defeat, and ruin, but the confession and forsaking of sin will bring merciful pardon and relief' (Adams, 1970 p. 105).

The premise for being out of control is sin; sin keeps a veil up between GOD and us. When sin is present in our lives, we keep GOD from blessing us and then we are in a whirl spin; constantly turning around, not being able to stop and focus. Non-confessed sin keeps us off the road and we have no sense of direction. We want to stop spinning but we cannot, we are trapped until we realize that we need to get right with GOD. In addition, confessing sin would relieve us from stress and as well.

After we get right with GOD, then the next thing we should do is make it right with our brother or sister we wronged. However, we would do well to rehearse what we are going to say before we go to them. 'Man-Up' to whatever we did, meaning do not take any cope-outs or allow the other person to down play your action(s). This also gives spiritual relief from stress and pressure when we make things right with people that we wronged. We are commanded to forgive one another and in turn, GOD will forgive us.

GOD'S ROADMAP:

One of the next things we should do is recognize the problem and the pressure. Elizabeth Brown states, "That is the problem in a difficult relationship: If you didn't care, it would not make any difference what someone did or did not do. It would be irrelevant. Not caring, you could stand back, assess the problem, ascertain the possibilities, and devise a plan for successful survival. You understand what you need, and you long to move toward your goals. However, the externals – friends, family, commitments, duties, and responsibilities – conflict with your objectives. Caring makes you feel pulled in different directions. It's like being directionless" (Brown, p.24). I disagree with the point that we should not allow anyone to keep us from our goals. The key is our faith in GOD, for we can do all things through CHRIST who strengthens us. In addition, if the LORD is our Shepherd, then he guides and leads us so we always have a sense of direction by following CHRIST. There should not be any stress and pressure if we put things in God's hand and leave it there.

However, Elizabeth Brown mentions, "Good mental health depends on discernment that assesses the situation, determines options, and moves on, even though we care. Don't allow the pressure to force you into compliance with behavior that: is wrong, goes against your beliefs, would squash someone's spirit, and is immoral" (Brown, p.25). I totally agree; when feeling pressured, stand on our beliefs, and remember what thus says the LORD. GOD is the ultimate judge on whether we will have victory and/or make it through our situations.

When we are spinning out of control, it may seem as if we are going in every direction possible, but this is not the case. One thing we need to do is grab hold of the steering wheel, and press down on the brake not slam on them. When we are spinning out of control, we have no sense of gravity or where we are. The steering wheel controls the direction of where we are trying to go, but that is not the only thing we have to worry about. We still have to stop spinning, which means we have to take back control over our life.

To take control back over our lives, we first have to realize that we were out of control. Seek GOD for help, it is written that man cannot live by bread alone. We must get some help. Trying to do things on our own may seem like the best thing to do, but we are at our weakest point when we try. One twig could be easily snapped and broken; but a hand full of twigs can- not be so easily snapped and/or broken. There is great strength in numbers, and we must realize this and seek help through varies people. Remember to pray over our situation and let GOD direct our steps. GOD may work through other people, so be open to receive help when it comes; it just may be from the LORD. It is very helpful to be in constant prayer, especially when we are going through. GOD will grant us an answer. At times, it may not be what we want to hear; however, when GOD gives us an answer it is always good for us.

Do not play the blaming game. Blaming others for our problems never solves our situation. The blaming game has been since the beginning with Adam and Eve in the Garden of Eden. Adam blamed Eve and Eve blamed Satan. However, no one took ownership for their particular problem in their life – sin. It did not work then, and it will not work now. We must take responsibility for our actions. We are behind the wheel and no one else. Therefore, we must take responsibility for our own actions, and seek God's forgiveness.

Beware of the enemy inside ourselves – us! We are our own worst enemy. When man does not follow and obey GOD, man is left to his own devices. This is the worst possible place to be. We are just there, with no sign and no presence of GOD in our lives. We are lost and spinning out of control. GOD is needed in our lives to bring order to chaos. When we try to convince ourselves that we are not as bad off as you think, then once again, we deceive ourselves. Man has portrayed an ego problem since the beginning. Ever since man desired to be wise as GOD, man has been forever hoodwinked in that thinking. GOD is the only Supreme Being and man is not even close to His glory or knowledge.

Now we must reduce the stress and pressure in our lives. Many people are becoming mentally, physically, and spiritually ill becomes of the stress and pressure in their life.

There will always be stress and pressure in life. Some people handle the stress and pressure of life well, and others do not. GOD never said that we would not have trials and tribulations in life. Actually, GOD said that it rains on the just and unjust just the same. That means - whether we are His child or not, we will have stress and pressure in life, but the key is if we are His children, GOD will never leave us nor forsake us. All we have to do is turn to Him and live by His commandments.

Dealing with Life's Pressures

When people are spinning out of control due to the stress and pressures of life, they respond and deal with it very differently. Some deal with stress and pressure by involving themselves with external sources, which could be negative and have negative consequences such as gambling, sexual entertainment, drinking, drugs, and criminal activity.

Nevertheless, how do Active Christians deal with stress and pressures of life? They pray – primarily, prayer changes things. Instead of being beaten up with worrying about life's stress and pressures, Active Christians put their faith and trust in the LORD. Trusting in the LORD gives you a peace that surpasses all understanding. Christians also meditate on God's WORD, and in doing this we can fight the need to worry about problems and stress and pressures of life. Active Christians also praise and worship GOD no matter their current situation.

In addition, along with prayer and meditation, Active Christians should exercise to reduce their stress and pressure level. By exercising, we can release built up tension in our minds and our bodies can give off chemicals; a release that calms us down, and reduces the stress and pressure levels. For all the married couples, making love helps to reduce stress and pressure levels. Keep in mind what having sex could do. It brings us closer with our spouse who reminds us that we are not alone as we are going through. Next, it releases hormones that could calm you down after a climax. Lastly, it is a form of exercise itself. Afterwards, you could be very tired and ready to go to sleep.

I also suggest working on something you enjoy doing. For many people, I included, this means we enjoy doing work in our profession. This is something I enjoy doing, I do not see work as work, it is quite enjoyable, so if we enjoy doing work then do it! Do whatever we can do that is consider stress free.

Having fun with family could be a great stress relief as well. I play video games with my family. We play card games such as Uno, Phase 10, and Spades. We all are highly competitive, and after several rounds, we tend to forget all about the stress and pressures we are facing-- especially when we are playing the games. Our games are very challenging, and we try our hardest to have fun, while still trying to win at all cost. At that point, what are the problems? Life seems to be back in focus and we are fellowshipping with friends and family.

Working in the Ministry always is a great way to reduce the stress and pressure. When we are about God's business, he will be about ours. God's Word says, "It's better to give than receive." When we are working in the ministry, we honor GOD by trusting in Him and serving Him as well. We could never go wrong in serving GOD and doing His Will. We just have to stay obedient to GOD at all times. Normally, when we are going through hard times, we tend to seek GOD the most. Sometimes I wonder why we cry to GOD when things are going wrong more than when they are going good, and all GOD desires is praise and worship. Maybe that is one of the reasons why we experience trials and tribulations; to keep us in constant fellowship with GOD.

Renewing our Purpose:

Upon the completion of this chapter, we should know: when we are spinning out of control due to life's stress and pressures, GOD is still present in our lives. Remember, GOD will never leave us nor forsake us. This is the time to acknowledge the sin that is in our lives. Go to GOD in prayer, confess, and repent.

GOD'S ROADMAP:

Struggling with a Situation:

The stress and pressure is on, we feel like life has gotten to rough for us. We have tried to handle our problems by ourselves because we did not want to burden anyone else with our situation. Now we are feeling overwhelmed and we do not know what to do or where to turn. On the other hand, maybe we are stuck in the format of solving our problems; we know nothing different, and we are ready for some fresh revelations.

Reading the Proclaim:

"Be anxious for nothing, but in everything by prayer and supplication, with thanksgiving, let your requests be made known to GOD; and the peace of GOD, which surpasses all understanding, will guard your hearts and minds through CHRIST JESUS." (Philippians 4: 6-7)

Making our Routine Permanent: As we contemplate on this situation, let us be reminded:

When we worry about a problem or situation we are not trusting GOD, therefore we are in sin by not fully trusting in GOD to bring us through whatever trial we are facing. Remember that we are children of GOD and He loves and provides for us daily. Stress and pressure is on the rise, and many people are getting sick from it. Do not be a victim of stress and pressure; be victors over it.

Conducting a Righteous Project:

Take an inventory of the pressure in our life to see where our pressure pulse is placed.

Peterson's Pressure Point

Indicate how you feel with each statement on a scale from 0 to 4:

0 = never   1= rarely   2 = sometimes   3 = often   4 = always

_____ Always Tired
_____ Always want to hide
_____ Have trouble relaxing
_____ Bossy
_____ Always tense
_____ Always worried
_____ Lonely & Unwanted
_____ Moody
_____ Overwhelmed by responsibilities
_____ Lack of concentration
_____ Always anger
_____ Never satisfied
_____ Can't Eat
_____ Sense of Hopelessness
_____ Always Sick
_____ Can't sleep
_____ Indecisive
_____ Don't like being in charge
_____ Have a lack of trust of people
_____ See the glass as half filled
_____ Always procrastinating
_____ Have an I can do it by myself attitude
_____ Sense of Helplessness
_____ Always feeling stressed
_____ Always troubled

_____ Total

Scoring

70 – 100 Highly stress

50 – 69 Moderate stress

25 – 49 Mild stressed

0 – 24 Non significant

Meditating on a Reflective Prayer:

GOD, I am the problem forgive me for my disobedience. Strength me oh LORD only as you can. I can do nothing without you. I put my trust, my hope, and faith in you. Thank you for being my Father and my GOD. Amen.

Chapter 5: Full Speed Ahead

Now we are ready to move forward in life. We have taken responsibility for our mind, the way we feel, and what we do. Now we are ready to pursue happiness. Happiness is satisfaction and joy. One thing we must do is limit our focus. By doing this, we are no longer burden down with facing daily outside factors. Everyday new problems arise; we have to focus on what is before us and use our mental capacity to solve that problem. Do not become burden down with stress and pressure.

However, if we fail or cannot solve a problem, that in itself, is not failure. We can still experience success even in failure. We experience success "when we accept defeat and move forward with courage, we are choosing to stay on the path of success" (Diehm 1994, p.123). This will keep us on the right road heading towards JESUS.

We should constantly remind ourselves that we are the head and not the tail. We are of a royal priesthood. GOD has put in us everything we will need to be successful. Therefore, when things go astray, we must keep reminding ourselves that we are going to make it. Self-motivation is always a positive when we are trying to get our spirits up. "Faith is a mental attitude that is a prerequisite to problem-solving. The GOD and I can do it attitude is undefeatable in problem-solving" (Diehm 1994, p.130). A change of attitude could directly affect happiness in our lives. "The same is true for our future. When we invest in it wisely, we see greater dividends." (Omartian 2001, p.213) Active Christians do an excellent job locking into GOD and reciting His promises and blessings, He has for us.

As we continue to pass new surroundings, we are moving forward, we become motivated by the new possibilities that exist. We gain a spiritual high knowing that GOD has not forsaken us, and then our mental capacity begins to work overtime thinking ahead on the next turn. We are ready and excited for the next challenge in life.

GOD'S ROADMAP:

"There are so many scriptures that build us up in our minds. We begin to overflow with who we are in CHRIST. Get into the Word of GOD and gain wisdom into our spirit. No matter what our circumstances, the Word never changes" (Crouch 1998, p.72). Now that is encouragement! Thank you JESUS. Read 1 Peter 2:9 in your spare time.

The pursuit of happiness can also come from having a higher purpose in life. Once we become engaged with doing something greater than we do, it gives us a new out-look on life. We then need to organize our lives and do what is most important first. Make sure we keep GOD first in our lives. The bible states, "Seek first the kingdom of GOD and His righteousness, and all these things shall be added to you" (Matthew 6:33). Secondly, keep home happy. A happy spouse keeps our mental state happy and vibrant. Next, make sure we are enjoying what we are doing in life. If we are doing, what we enjoy, our attitude becomes pleasant, and the way we treat others will be reflected in the way we treat them. "Get your mind off the problems or circumstances in your life and onto the solution. Change your thinking from defeat to victory." (Crouch, 1998 p.65) Changing our mind set is very important. It is the first step in getting out of the hole we dug. If we can conceive it, then we can achieve it. We must first believe we can and then the rest will be easy because we believe.

When we place other people's needs before our own, we can get an inner glow knowing that we are doing the work of the LORD. We can look at a person in need as needing God's blessing, and GOD can bless them through us. "I have seen this kind of powerful impact time and again over the years. When the wealthy and the poor get together, each ends up meeting the desperate needs of the other. Too often Satan achieves his wicked agenda by keeping them apart – geographically and philosophically. The result is that one tends to die in need, the other in greed. However, when JESUS brings us together, the genuine needs of both are mysteriously and wonderfully satisfied. In God's amazing economy, the rich and poor need each other, the common message being, 'Enough really is … enough!" (Stafford 2007, p. 107) Spiritually, you will begin to feel better when you are blessing others. GOD gives us blessings to bless other people, and when things are going badly in our life, it is always refreshing to feel useful.

28

The next chapter is probably the most important chapter of the whole book. It deals with the art of letting go. This concept is so hard for many of us to master. We have to believe that we can get over whatever has us bound. My prayer is for all who read this chapter that all will find deliverance.

Renewing our Purpose:

Upon the completion of this chapter, we should know: that our mind is the battleground for spiritual warfare, and we must equip ourselves for battle. We need to encourage our happiness and ourselves in the LORD; for all battles will shine through no matter what our circumstances.

Struggling with a Situation:

Your life is out of order with GOD and your family. You have been drawn away from your fellowship with JESUS through deceptions and distractions. You do not feel like talking or doing activities with your family. The truth is, you are feeling depressed.

Reading the Proclaim:

"Many sorrows shall be to the wicked; but he who trusts in the LORD, mercy shall surround him. Be glad in the LORD and rejoice, you righteous; and shout for joy, all you upright in heart!" (Psalm 32:10-11)

Making our Routine Permanent: As we contemplate on this situation, let us be reminded.

That GOD is a jealous GOD, and we should not have anything or anyone before Him. Nor shall we bow down and serve anything other than GOD Himself. GOD desires a close intimate relationship with us, therefore, we must avail ourselves for worship and prayer daily.

Conducting a Righteous Project:

When you are about God's business, He will be about your business. Think of some ways in which you can bless someone other than yourself. Who is in need that you see daily? Now write down some things you could do to help them, then choose one and do it.

_____

_____

_____

_____

_____

_____

Meditating on a Reflective Prayer:

Father we thank you for first loving us. Help us to remain focused on You, JESUS. Please give us the heart to serve others. In JESUS' name, we pray. Amen.

Chapter   6: Yielding

Failing from time to time is a part of life, but failure is refusing to get back up or to get back in line with the Word of GOD. GOD has taught us how to deal with failure. JESUS told the disciples *"If people do not welcome you, shake the dust off your feet when you leave their town, as a testimony against them."* (Luke 9:5) This is how we should deal with failure and disappointments. JESUS wants us to move on, in other words, shift the car out of park and into drive. Failing and feeling rejected is something that we are supposed to expect according to GOD. Often we fall down but we must keep getting back up, and keep our eyes on JESUS. It rains on the just and unjust; meaning bad things are going to happen no matter what. We can- not continue to stay down being children of the GOD of the Most High. We are truly over- comers and we must act accordingly.

All believers have the Holy Spirit in them; we just need to walk in the Spirit, yielding to God's control. Meaning - we do not have to continue following our flesh. W e have the ability to let go things that we are stuck to. The Holy Spirit lets us know when we have gone down the wrong path, and helps us to get back on the right path, and stay on it.

God's WORD penetrates our hearts to up root the deepest sins. We have to meditate on God's Word day and night, and obey it. Make it a daily habit of studying God's Word and memorizing Scriptures. Use the power of prayer to overcome sin as well. JESUS says, "The Spirit is willing but the flesh is weak." Prayer humbles us to know that we are not able to do what GOD can only do. We pray to the Father for strength and power to overcome sin. Sin is not the only thing we are over-coming; we are also overcoming stress and pressure as well. Sin attacks us mentally, physically, and spiritually just like stress and pressure.

Become active in a bible teaching and preaching church where JESUS is taught as LORD and SAVIOR. We need the love of other believers to overcome sin as well. We learned that there is strength in numbers, so we need to surround ourselves with fellow Christians that can help cover us in our time of need. There is no shame in asking for help. Many times, people need an extra boost to make it through. Stress and pressure are two by-products from sin, and we need all the help we can get to overcome it all.

At times, we allow something that happened to us affect us so badly until we remain still - unable to move, unable to grow, and unable to believe. When we have a problem of letting go, we are stuck in park. Only when we realize that we are no longer moving can we then start seeking how to move forward. We all have had something in our lives that keep us stuck, and unable to move forward. We try to fix the problem ourselves, and therefore waste even more time being still when we could have been driving forward on the road.

Some people remain in park because they blame others for their disposition. They believe no one cares so they remain where they are. They often say no one is around to help point them in the right direc-tion. They often believe that others should be doing for them what they should be doing for themselves. We often blame others when they do not point us in the right direction, when in actuality, only GOD can do that. Being stuck in park is no one's fault but our own! We are respon-sible for our own lives. No one lives that life but us. Yes, bad things are going to happen; GOD foretold us this in His Word. We have to be ready to grow from it and accept responsibility for our own actions.

We are children of the All-knowing GOD; therefore, we can always tap into GOD for directions. GOD always knows the right road to take for our lives. We have to overcome the mental battle of think-ing that we are a no-body because we lost, or that we have failed at something. We have to stop reliving bad things that happened to us. Satan continues to try to keep us in an unmovable position.

He does not want us to get close to GOD; therefore, he will continue to try to distract us from keeping our eyes on JESUS. This is why we remain stuck. W e have to realize that GOD blesses us. Do not let stress and pressure dominate our way of thinking or the actions we take.

One concept from 'The Art of Letting Go' is confessing and repenting from our sins. Unless we face the sin that has us bound, we will remain stuck in park. Believe in JESUS CHRIST and accept Him as our personal LORD and SAVIOR. John 1:9 says, *"If we confess our sins, He is faithful and just to forgive us our sins and to cleanse us from all unrighteousness."* Confessing and repenting of sin is the only way to get rid of sin; when we do this, we also relieve ourselves from the issues of stress and pressure. Therefore, it is to our benefit mentally, physically, and spiritually to confess and repent from sin.

Often in our minds, we keep rehearsing bad things that have happened to us. We keep replaying that horrible event repeatedly in our minds. *"No weapon that forms against us shall prosper."* (Isaiah 54:17) Our childhood pains, our strong addictions, and past sins constantly tries to keep us distracted. Learn to worship JESUS when our minds seem stuck in the past. Our minds have become exhausted - needing to be relieved of all the poison we have allowed in it. To keep reliving bad events that happened causes undue stress and pressure on our body. This is one way people are becoming sick mentally, physically, and spiritually. People begin to break down because they cannot move past events that have happened. This type of situation takes much prayer to overcome it. We must cling to our prayer language.

GOD'S ROADMAP:

When someone has been suppressed for so long, they need to grab hold to something, and that something is Hope. After you have done something very wrong, or have sinned terribly, we need to know that GOD still offers hope to us. All people have sinned throughout the bible, starting with Adam in the Garden of Eden, but GOD still offered Hope to Adam. GOD told him that a SAVIOR would come through Eve. God's great news gave Adam hope. It also gave man Hope! The hope is for all God's children to have everlasting life through JESUS CHRIST. Not to have hope is a form of stress and pressure. It suffocates us internally and externally. People must have something to believe in, and not experience the form of hopelessness.

Everyone needs hope, especially when he or she has been stuck in park for so long that they forgot how to let go. However, the good news is that they can be set free through CHRIST JESUS. We can get back on the road rolling again. Often people get burden down with sin; especially those personal sins that we have a hard time admitting and walking away from. We need to know that we can always take our sins and problems to JESUS. Only GOD has the power to forgive us of all our sins, so why keep being tormented. Learn the art of letting go by confessing and repenting to GOD. It is time to start living a stress-free life, or start living a less stressful life.

Once the situation is done... it is done. Just like in football, when that down is over it's a new down whether we go from 1st to 2nd, 2nd to 3rd, or 3rd to 4th. Once that down is over, it is over. Whether that down was successful enough to get us, a new set of downs or not, it is over. Learn to focus on the next down. In real life terms, learn to focus on the next situation in life. Therefore, whether we just went through a bitter divorce, life still goes on. Now focus on life without that particular person in it. GOD still sits high and looks low and He loves us. GOD will never leave us nor forsake us. Focus on rebuilding our relationship with JESUS and let Him be the foundation for our new life. Once we are pass the past, we are past it. What does it matter if we done one thing wrong or a hundred things wrong? GOD still has the power to forgive us from it all. We just let it go and move on.

Renewing our Purpose:

Upon the completion of this chapter, we should know: that GOD has traffic signs in place to help direct where we need to go. GOD cares for us like any good father, and wants to lead us to Him. Look for signs that points to JESUS and follow that path. GOD is always there and waiting on us to resume our journey on the road that leads to Him.

Struggling with a Situation:

Something of great value has been taken from you. You have been accustomed to having this in your life for years. Now you have to move on without it, and you do not know how. You are now facing a divorce or a break-up. Life goes on! It does not matter that they are no longer in your life; GOD still loves you and desires a close intimate relationship with you.

Reading the Proclaim:

"These things I have spoken unto you, that in me ye might have peace. In the world ye shall have tribulation: but be of good cheer; I have overcome the world." (John 16:33)

Making our Routine Permanent: As we contemplate on this situation, let us be reminded:

That disconnecting from what we are use to is vital for moving on with our lives. Being use to a person, a job, or a situation is normal. However, when it is lost or taken away, we act as if we do not know how to move on. We have to learn how to give it to GOD. Lay our burdens upon JESUS because he cares for us. Then, disconnect from it emotionally. At times, we can be so wrapped up into that situation until all we see, is what use to be there. Once it is gone, it is time for us to move on. Let Go! Life is full of changes - it happens every single day. One moment its light, then darkness the next, but the sun will shine again! We just have to realize this and stay encouraged.

Conducting a Righteous Project:

With this exercise, we will practice letting go and seeing what is current in our life:

I was use to being _____

I am no longer _____

I am better now that it is gone because _____

I am still a child of _____

GOD loves me & I am His _____

GOD will never leave me nor _____

GOD has blessed me with _____

I am alive and _____

There is a possibility for me to _____

I love myself more than _____

I deserve to be happy and filled _____

Meditating on a Reflective Prayer:

Heavenly Father, we thank you for looking beyond our faults and you have the heart to love us even when we do not love ourselves, as we should. Help us to be better than we are. In Jesus' name, we pray. Amen.

Chapter 7: Going the Right Direction

Once we lock our eyes on JESUS, we are headed in the right direction. Therefore, whatever obstacles we may encounter, GOD has the power to see us through it. GOD has the power to make the smallest thing in our life mighty. This should give us a sense of hope and encouragement.

GOD gives us renewed hope through JESUS CHRIST. GOD loves us and He constantly points us in the right direction. No matter how lost we are; we have hope in JESUS! Man has hope that he can overcome misery, hardships, and being lost thru JESUS CHRIST. JESUS has defeated sin and all that it entails. Therefore, there is no need for us to stress over any situation. Stand up and put a smile on that face; GOD is still in the blessing business!

Grace is God's kindness bestowed upon man even the undeserving. It is granted to sinners, pardoning them of their sins, and affords man eternal salvation through JESUS CHRIST. When we are driving in the right direction, we are experiencing God's grace. No amount of stress and pressure should be able to derail us! GOD is powerful than ANY Situation! We must believe it and accept that our GOD is ALL MIGHTY!

Grace is getting what we do not deserve. We may have been a poor navigator of the car of life we are driving, but GOD still wants to direct us to Himself. Grace is not being condemned to hell. We all have sinned and we all have come up short of the glory of GOD. GOD still offers us salvation through JESUS CHRIST, which is grace to have everlasting life with Him. When we are driving towards JESUS, in life, we may go down many dangerous roads, and we may be stuck at times. Grace is the power of GOD that gets us out of the mess and traps that we could not get out of by ourselves. God's Grace covers us and NOTHING can overpower that! Therefore, we should never lose hope, nor have a defeated attitude.

When we are stuck from time to time, some of us panic and get nervous because we cannot move. Be still and know He is GOD; maybe GOD does not want us to move. Have we ever considered that? GOD does whatever he wants to do for His Glory. No one knows the mind of GOD. If we are not moving, GOD has his divine reason why we are at a standstill. Use this opportunity to praise and worship GOD; doing this will lift our spirits.

GOD wants to give us all that can be afforded to us. We just have to diligently seek Him and obey His voice. We have to keep GOD first and work hard towards Him and His commandments. We have to learn how to keep moving towards JESUS - even when we go down dark roads with our vision impaired. This is a perfect time to activate our faith in CHRIST, and drive by faith and not by sight.

When it is your season, GOD will orchestrate people to be a blessing when you need additional help. Be the leader GOD called you to be. GOD has given you favor to receive everything he intends to give you. Embrace GOD and receive your gifts. Set your eyes on GOD, put your foot on the gas, and move towards Him. Forget the wrong turns you made in life, once GOD has revealed your path then, focus on that only moving towards GOD.

Renewing our Purpose:

Upon the completion of this chapter, we should know: that we are blessed; and GOD is the key to relieving the stress and pressure of life. We should praise GOD even in time of prosperity. Always give glory and honor to GOD. We must discipline ourselves to give GOD thanks for everything, especially the good. GOD gives us blessings and we must not find it robbery-honoring GOD for His Goodness and for His Faithfulness.

Struggling with a Situation:

You are finally out of a dark, hard, and painful situation. Everything seems to be going your way. Have you thanked GOD for your deliverance? Have you praised GOD for bringing us out of our deep, dark, and empty hole? Have you forgotten to give honor to the Father? Now is the time to lift Holy hands and praise Him.

Reading the Proclaim:

"And it shall come to pass, if ye shall hearken diligently unto my commandments which I command you this day, to love the LORD your GOD, and to serve Him with all your heart and with all your soul, That I will give you the rain of your land in his due season, the first rain and the latter rain, that thou mayest gather in thy corn, and thy wine, and thine oil. And I will send grass in thy fields for thy cattle, that thou mayest eat and be full." (Deuteronomy 11:13-15)

Making our Routine Permanent: As we contemplate on this situation let us be reminded.

Without the grace, without the pardon that God gives us, we will die. GOD supplies us daily with the light of the sun and air to breath, something to eat, and drink. He supplies all we need, but we must choose to accept His gifts, or to reject them.

Conducting a Righteous Project:

Write a personal thank you note to GOD for all His many blessings in your life. Tell Him thank you for his Grace and Mercy. Let GOD know how you could not have made it without Him.

_____

_____

_____

_____

Reflective Prayer:

LORD JESUS, I know you have a plan for my life. I need your guidance to direct my path. Strengthen me in my time of need. I cannot make it without you. In JESUS' name, I pray. Amen.

Survey

Establishing Goals

The Pressure Awareness Christian Survey (PACS) was used to determine the amount of stress and pressure Active Christians deal with compared to the Average Person.

What percentage is the affect on the mental, spiritual, and physical aspect of the human body when one rely on JESUS CHRIST as their personal LORD and SAVIOR compared to the average person who may or may not be an Active Christian.

What percentage of Active Christian people responds differently from the Average Person when dealing with stress and pressure?

What is the percentage in the benefits of having JESUS CHRIST as a personal LORD and SAVIOR compared to not having Him as LORD and SAVIOR?

What percentage of people's health increased from the benefits of JESUS CHRIST as their personal LORD and SAVIOR compared to not having Him?

The survey consists of 20 questions that give insight on spiritual, mental, and physical ways people respond to stress and pressure.

Participants were 100 people total, 50 from 2 local churches, and 50 from a local mall and a local college. The groups are based on two categories one representing 50 people being Active Christians, the other category representing 50 Average People coming from a local mall and a local college campus. The 50 people representing the Average People may or may not be an Active Christian.

The findings from this study may reveal the benefits of having CHRIST as a personal LORD and SAVIOR. Non-religious people, especially the age bracket of 18 – 28, may be the people demonstrating the highest levels of stress and pressure. Also this is in line with "College students, especially freshmen, are a group particularly prone to stress (D'Zurilla & Sheedy, 1991) due to the transitional nature of college life. They must adjust to being away from home for the first time, maintain a high level of academic achievement, and adjust to a new social environment. College students, regardless of year in school, often deal with pressures related to finding a job or a potential life partner." (Hirsch, J. K., & Ellis, J. B. 1996)

The amount of stress and pressure experienced by people may be greatly influenced by their religious beliefs and the way they respond to stressful events. People respond to stress and pressure differently, however, allowing GOD to enter into your life and make light your burdens could greatly reduce your stress and pressure level. This study examined perceptions of having CHRIST in your life and living according to the WORD of GOD compared to the possibility of not living accordingly to the WORD of GOD, and the stress level that may arise.

Introduction:

Stress and pressure among human beings is nothing new; however, the difference between an Active Christian versus the Average Person has not been studied in depth. This study will give deeper insight between the comparisons between the two groups. There have been many studies on "College students experience high stress at predictable times each semester due to academic commitments, financial pressures, and lack of time management skills. When stress is perceived negatively or becomes excessive, it can affect both health performance" (Misra, McKean, West, & Russo 2000).

This study examined (1) the affect on the mental, spiritual, and physical aspect of the human body when one relies on JESUS CHRIST as their personal LORD and SAVIOR, compared to the Average Person who may or may not be an Active Christian; (2) used to determine the amount of stress and pressure active Christians deal with compared to the Average person.; (3) benefits of having JESUS CHRIST as a personal LORD and SAVIOR compared to not having Him as LORD and SAVIOR. In addition, there may be a difference between men and women, and how they perceive stress and pressure.

Method:

Sample Design, Survey, and Data Collection were used.

The sample consisted of two major components. Component 1 consisted of Active Christians from two churches. Participants in Group one were 50 people (23 males, 27 females) from the two churches. One church was Fellowship @ Midway in Midway, FL and the second church was Tabernacle Missionary Baptist in Tallahassee, FL. Information was collected using a survey. I went to various people and asked them if they would complete a random survey for a study, I was conducting for my dissertation. They were allowed to put the survey in a fabricated drop box. My success rate of having all to fill out the survey and turn it back in was 100%.

Component 2 also consisted of the same survey used with two different groups. Group one was 20 full-time students (freshmen) at Florida State University in Tallahassee, Florida. Group two was 30 random people at the Tallahassee Mall. Participants in component two were 50 people (17 males, 33 females) from the two separate groups. My success rate of getting 30 people to fill out the survey and turn it in was 100%.

Materials and Procedures:

The Pressure Awareness Christian Survey (PACS) was created by Ron Peterson to look at the differences between people who trusted JESUS CHRIST and followed him to people who may not, and the differences between stress and pressure that both groups reported. The survey consisted of 20 questions that were divided into three different types of stress and pressure: 10 questions responded to spiritual, 5 questions responded to physical, and 5 responded to mental stress. The response format was (all the time, most of the time, some of the time, and none of the time) and (poor, fair, good, and excellent).

Basic demographic information was collected on age, gender, and religious affiliations.

GOD'S ROADMAP:

Here is a copy of the actual survey.

Pressure Awareness Christian's Survey (PACS)

How would you rate yourself?
Active Christian   Inactive Christian other religion no religion
   18-28   29-43   44-59   60-Up (Age)

Gender: [ ] male   [ ] female

Directions: Mark one box per question.

Part I. Spiritual

1. How often do you pray?
   All the Time   Most of the Time   Some of the Time   None of the Time

2. How often do you rely on GOD to solve your problems?
   All the Time   Most of the Time   Some of the Time   None of the Time

3. How often do you attend church?
   All the Time   Most of the Time   Some of the Time   None of the Time

4. How often do you meditate on God's Word about your situation?
   All the Time   Most of the Time   Some of the Time   None of the Time

5. How often do you rely on yourself to get out of your problems?
   All the Time   Most of the Time   Some of the Time   None of the Time

6. How often do you ask others for help?
   All the Time   Most of the Time   Some of the Time   None of the Time

7. How often do you limit your focus on the concerns of the day?
   All the Time   Most of the Time   Some of the Time   None of the Time

8. How often do you have a feeling of emptiness?
   All the Time   Most of the Time   Some of the Time   None of the Time

9. How often do you look for a magical solution for your problems?
   All the Time   Most of the Time   Some of the Time   None of the Time

10. How often are you at peace about your problems?
   All the Time   Most of the Time   Some of the Time   None of the Time

Part II. Physical

11. When you are dealing with your problems, how often do you experience anxiety?
   All the Time   Most of the Time   Some of the Time   None of the Time

12. How often do you get migraine headaches?
   All the Time   Most of the Time   Some of the Time   None of the Time

13. How often do you get sick?
   All the Time   Most of the Time   Some of the Time   None of the Time

14. How often do you exercise?
   All the Time   Most of the Time   Some of the Time   None of the Time

15. How often do you eat nutritious meals?
   All the Time   Most of the Time   Some of the Time   None of the Time

Part III. Mental

16. When things don't go accordingly to plan, how often do you remind yourself its normal?
   All the Time   Most of the Time   Some of the Time   None of the Time

17. How do you feel about yourself?
   Poor   Fair   Good   Excellent

18. How do you feel that your life is going?
   Poor   Fair   Good   Excellent

19. How often is your mind busy?
   All the Time   Most of the Time   Some of the Time   None of the Time

20. How often do you feel pressure from your commitments?
   All the Time   Most of the Time   Some of the Time   None of the Time

Results and Discussion:

100 people (P= 100) were analyzed to address three questions:

1) Are non-active Christians prone to experience higher levels of stress?

2) Is there a relationship between stress and pressure and following JESUS?

3) Do stressed people experience lower levels of mental, physical, and spiritual wellness?

I found that the Average Person in today's society is more stressed than the active Christian. The Average Person in Today's society is less likely to participate in exercising, and is more prone to headaches and other physical forms of stress. People under greater stress and pressure also exhibit lower levels of self-esteem.

There were three categories that were addressed: the mental, physical, and spiritual. The distribution of responses was as follows: 50% of the stressors were spiritual, 25% were physical, and 25% were mental. These are the results from the survey according to frequency of what the 100 people selected.

Table 1 Frequency of responses to each question. You will be able to see the number of Active Christians and the Average Person selections, along with the all-100 people and their selections. There were several questions that stood out in an interesting point of view. There were percentages that were extremely high when you know the category in spiritual more so than the other two. It is good to know that most people are praying people based on the data. However, it does not register if you are not a child of GOD. GOD only hears the prayers of the righteous. It would be beneficial if the people who were not born-again believers to accept the LORD JESUS and become His children; then and only then could you be afforded all the benefits that comes from being His child.

Frequency

How often do you pray?

All the Time	Most of the Time	Some of the Time	None of the Time
40 T 11 AP 29 AC	26 T 10 AP 16 AC	31 T 26 AP 5 AC	3 T 3 AP 0 AC

How often do you rely on GOD to solve your problems?

All the Time	Most of the Time	Some of the Time	None of the Time
27 T 6 AP 21 AC	45 T 20 AP 25 AC	19 T 15 AP 4 AC	9 T 9 AP 0 AC

How often do you attend church?

All the Time	Most of the Time	Some of the Time	None of the Time
46 T 8 AP 38 AC	25 T 13 AP 12 AC	19 T 19 AP 0 AC	10 T 10 AP 0 AC

How often do you mediate on God's Word about your situation?

All the Time	Most of the Time	Some of the Time	None of the Time
20 T 9 AP 11 AC	47 T 13 AP 34 AC	24 T 19 AP 5 AC	9 T 9 AP 0 AC

Going the Right Direction

How often do you rely on yourself to get out of your problems?

All the Time	Most of the Time	Some of the Time	None of the Time
12 T 10 AP 2 AC	37 T 25 AP 12 AC	40 T 10 AP 30 AC	11 T 5 AP 6 AC

How often do you ask others for help?

All the Time	Most of the Time	Some of the Time	None of the Time
4 T 3 AP 1 AC	28 T 24 AP 4 AC	59 T 16 AP 43 AC	9 T 7 AP 2 AC

How often do you limit your focus on the concerns of the day?

All the Time	Most of the Time	Some of the Time	None of the Time
1 T 1 AP 0 AC	32 T 11 AP 21 AC	52 T 25 AP 27 AC	15 T 13 AP 2 AC

How often do you have a feeling of emptiness?

All the Time	Most of the Time	Some of the Time	None of the Time
3 T 3 AP 0 AC	8 T 6 AP 2 AC	67 T 28 AP 39 AC	22 T 13 AP 9 AC

How often do you look for a magical solution for your problems?

All the Time	Most of the Time	Some of the Time	None of the Time
2 T 1 AP 1 AC	5 T 5 AP 0 AC	21 T 18 AP 3 AC	72 T 26 AP 46 AC

How often are you at peace about your problems?

All the Time	Most of the Time	Some of the Time	None of the Time
7 T 2 AP 5 AC	43 T 13 AP 30 AC	41 T 26 AP 15 AC	9 T 9 AP 0 AC

When you are dealing with your problems, how often do you experience anxiety?

All the Time	Most of the Time	Some of the Time	None of the Time
4 T 4 AP 0 AC	28 T 12 AP 16 AC	55 T 24 AP 31 AC	13 T 10 AP 3 AC

How often do you get migraine headaches?

All the Time	Most of the Time	Some of the Time	None of the Time
2 T 1 AP 1 AC	5 T 4 AP 1 AC	45 T 24 AP 21 AC	48 T 20 AP 28 AC

How often do you get sick?

All the Time	Most of the Time	Some of the Time	None of the Time
2 T 0 AP 2 AC	7 T 5 AP 2 AC	61 T 32 AP 29 AC	30 T 13 AP 17 AC

How often do you exercise?

All the Time	Most of the Time	Some of the Time	None of the Time
6 T 1 AP 5 AC	20 T 13 AP 7 AC	52 T 27 AP 25 AC	22 T 9 AP 13 AC

How often do you eat nutritious meals?

All the Time	Most of the Time	Some of the Time	None of the Time
7 T 6 AP 1 AC	53 T 17 AP 36 AC	32 T 19 AP 13 AC	8 T 8 AP 0 AC

When things don't go accordingly to plan, how often do you remind yourself its normal?

All the Time	Most of the Time	Some of the Time	None of the Time
6 T 3 AP 3 AC	37 T 10 AP 27 AC	46 T 27 AP 19 AC	11 T 10 AP 1 AC

GOD'S ROADMAP:

How do you feel about yourself?
Excellent	Good	Fair	Poor
28 T 10 AP 18 AC	62 T 31 AP 31 AC	8 T 7 AP 1 AC	2 T 2 AP 0 AC

How do you feel that your life is going?
Excellent	Good	Fair	Poor
22 T 8 AP 14 AC	63 T 30 AP 33 AC	15 T 12 AP 3 AC	0 T 0 AP 0 AC

How often is your mind busy?
All the Time	Most of the Time	Some of the Time	None of the Time
12 T 1 AP 11 AC	41 T 17 AP 24 AC	46 T 31 AP 15 AC	1 T 1 AP 0 AC

How often do you feel pressure from your commitments?
All the Time	Most of the Time	Some of the Time	None of the Time
11 T 3 AP 8 AC	28 T 10 AP 18 AC	52 T 21 AP 31 AC	9 T 3 AP 6 AC

The T represents the total of responses per indicator to each question, the AP represents the Average Person's response, and the AC represents the Active Christians' responses. Now let us take a closer look at the data to see what the data is showing us. In table 2 thru 4, Active Christians' data is being compared to the Average People's data. We will see distinct differences in how they deal with circumstances and experience similar situations, with CHRIST being the variable that is different for some and the same for others.

Table 2 compares Active Christians to the Average People and how they deal with stress and pressure from a spiritual point of view. The results are in percentages for each group based on all the time to most often data. AC represents Active Christians and AP represents the Average Person.

Table 2:

Spiritual Perspective   AC   AP

	AC	AP
More often to all the time pray to GOD.	90%	42%
More often to all the time rely on GOD to solve problems.	92%	52%
More often to all the time attends church.	100%	42%
More often to all the time mediate on God's WORD.	90%	44%
More likely to seldom experience feeling emptiness.	96%	62%

Table 3 compares Active Christians to the Average People and how they deal with stress and pressure from a physical point of view. The results are in percentages for each group based on all the time to most often data. AC represents Active Christians and AP represents the Average Person.

Table 3:

Physical Perspective	AC	AP
More often to all the time eating a nutritious meal.	74%	46%

Table 4 compares Active Christians to the Average People and how they deal with stress and pressure from a mental point of view. The results are in percentages for each group based on all the time to most often data. AC represents Active Christians and AP represents the Average Person.

Table 4:

Mental Perspective	AC	AP
More often to all the time realizing when bad things happen it is normal.	60%	26%
More often to all the time feeling that life is going good.	94%	76%
More likely to seldom experience pressure from commitments	74%	48%

Conclusion:

My results and findings support my hypotheses that there will be a tremendous decrease in stress and pressure for active Christians using techniques that GOD outlined in His Word. My results indicated a considerable reduction in stress and pressure that Active Christians experienced compared to the Average Person. The difference between the Active Christian and the Average Person is simply GOD. When people decides to live by God's means they experience less stress and pressure in their lives compared to the Average Person who may not be living accordingly to God's commandments.

Here are some of my results taken from the survey that was done comparing Active Christians to the Average Person. Note the degrees and percentages of the differences between both groups:

90% of Active Christians compared to 42% of the Average Person is more likely to pray to GOD to help them with their problems. Therefore, their stress and pressure level is down in comparison. Active Christians uses faith to help them relieve stress and pressure.

92% of Active Christians compared to 52% of the Average Person are more likely to rely on GOD to solve their problems. Therefore, Active Christians experience less stress and pressure than the average person does. Active Christians are less prone to continue dwelling in spiritual lows. I am not saying that Active Christians do not experience spiritual lows because they do. However, they know how and where to go to get that off them it is called JESUS CHRIST.

100% of Active Christians attend church compared to 42% of the Average Person that do not. Going to church is where people can go to get instruction, divine healing, and or a sense of purpose. Active Christians experience less stress and pressure because they come to the house of GOD and hear the Word of GOD that can break any stronghold that they may be experiencing in life.

90% of Active Christians meditate on God's WORD compared to 44% of the Average Person that does not. Realizing GOD has blessings for you and I that is encouragement in itself. Along with that, GOD has spoke promises and blessings for all of His children. Understanding what GOD has for you helps lift your spirits even when you are down.

96% of Active Christians almost never experience a feeling of emptiness compared to 62% of the Average Person that does. Whenever you have CHRIST in your life and the Spirit of GOD inside you, you are NEVER alone. When things look bleak and dark, all we have to do is tap inside ourselves where the HOLY SPIRIT dwells. We have a true power source if we use it. Active Christians are aware of this power more often than the Average Person, and therefore, have less pressure and stress.

74% of Active Christians eat nutritious meals compared to 46% of the Average Person that does not. Active Christians know the benefits of having a nutritious diet. GOD has outlined a healthy way of living in His WORD. We must remember this and live accordingly.

60% of Active Christians realizes when things go badly that it is normal compared to 26% of the Average Person that does not. GOD said in His WORD that it rains on the just and the unjust alike. When you read and study God's WORD, Scripture is clear that we will have trials and tribulations, but GOD will be with you until the end of the world.

94% of Active Christians feels that life is good compared to 76% of the Average Person that does. GOD is good all the time; all the time GOD is good! When you have GOD in your life, your life takes on a new meaning; you are able to see the joys of GOD throughout the world. Therefore, no matter how bad things are going it is only temporary. GOD is still in control and everything will work out for your good.

74% of Active Christians almost never experience pressure from commitments compared to 48% of the Average Person that does. We must not be anxious for nothing, and we should keep a calm head on every situation. We must realize that GOD is in control and He has it. There is no need to stress over any situation or feel pressure from commitments. All we have to do is tap into JESUS and He will see us through it all.

Personal Thoughts

GOD has given us a personal 'Road Map' in dealing with life's pressure and stress. We must trust GOD in all that He says and do in our life. We can live a less stressful life by obeying GOD and living in His statues and commandments. When we fail to live accordingly to God's law, we open ourselves up for all kinds of stress and pressure.

Prayer changes things! Instead of stressing over our daily problems, we should go to GOD in prayer. God's Word tells us to be anxious for nothing, and that the peace of GOD surpasses all understanding.

We have Scripture to meditate on when we are going through. We must realize we have an out from all stress and pressure we face every day in life. JESUS says, "Come to me, all of you who are weary and carry heavy burdens, and I will give you rest. Take my yoke upon you. Let me teach you, because I am humble and gentle, and you will find rest for your souls. For my yoke fits perfectly, and the burden I give you is light (Matthew 11:28-30). GOD gives us a peace of mind and heart, which is not of the world but of Him who has, overcame the world. Therefore, understanding and knowing we are not defeated by our problems. The victory is already won we have to trust in that.

We must continue to praise GOD even in the midst of our storms. GOD desires praise and worship, and when we take our eyes off ourselves and place them on JESUS, then, we free ourselves from personal bondage and hell we are currently going through. GOD is much larger than our problems. We serve a big GOD, a Mighty GOD, Mighty in Power and Majesty.

Life is full of stress and we cannot avoid it all. We have so much to do in life: we are husbands, wives, fathers, mothers, supervisors, employees, and brothers and sisters in CHRIST. There are tons of stress and pressures every single day. The key is not to trust in our self to do it all, but by trusting in GOD to give us strength, wisdom, and the power to do it all.

When we do this, we take up Christ's yoke because His yoke is easy and His burdens are light.

My hope is that my dissertation would cause many to focus on JESUS when dealing with stress and pressure. Man is made up of three parts; man has a body, a soul, and a spirit. Therefore, when we deal with man, we have to deal with the whole man and therefore, my research deals with the whole man in a spiritual, physical, and mental point of view. One of my challenges would be to get people to expand their thinking of trying to solve their problems all by themselves. GOD says, "Cursed is the man who trust in man and makes flesh his strength, whose heart departs from the LORD." (Jeremiah 17:10). GOD alone wants to be whom we turn to in time of need. That means stress and pressure of everyday life we need to turn to CHRIST; anything else we do will result in a curse.

There are many productive ways to deal with everyday stress and pressure. However, we have to learn how to place all of our cares on the LORD because he cares for us. I want to highlight effective ways in releasing stress and pressure.

Goals

❖ Provide Godly counsel to all people who are burden down with stress and pressure through this book God's Road Map: Mentally Releasing the Pressure.

❖ Provide spiritual counsel to all people in a counseling setting (contract with various churches and conduct seminars on stress and pressure).

❖ Provide stress and pressure relief counseling/faith based training to all churches throughout the world

❖ Create workshops/books/manuals that provide people, as well as helpers, with education about stress and pressure.

❖ After reading this book, people will use JESUS as their stress relief and use some healthy habits in dealing with pressure.

I do not want to conclude that children of GOD do not experience stress and pressure, actually; there is an article that shows the increase in ministers. Rev. Fred Wooden remembers when ministers use to preach, keep the congregation into it, and do weddings and funerals.

"The pressure to perform has gone up," said Wooden, whose three decades in the ministry include five years as senior minister of Fountain Street Church in downtown Grand Rapids. "But the financial resources to create performance have not gone up."

The foray into multitasking often includes futilely trying to meet hundreds, sometimes thousands, of people's expectations, continual fundraising campaigns, juggling bookkeeping and administrative responsibilities, and chairing one too many committees.

The pressure to perform is showing its detrimental side. Recent studies indicate clergy have more stress-related health problems than the general population and work longer hours — an average of 51 hours a week, according to one study.

In what researchers say is the largest and most detailed comparison of the health of clergy with that of the general population, Duke University's Clergy Health Initiative found in a study published in July that United Methodist Church ministers in North Carolina had higher-than-average rates of obesity, diabetes, blood pressure, asthma and arthritis.

The Rev. John Smith, national and regional director of Pastor Care, The National Clergy Support Network, said too many ministers have too much heaped on them, but few have the training or aptitude to fulfill all that is expected of them.

Compounding the problem is a sense of isolation ministers may feel because they are reluctant to reach out and discuss their troubles, triggering them to withdraw from friends and family, said Smith." (Kopenkoskey)

Active Christians need to understand that they to need to take time away from serving. GOD mentions rest and we are to do it. It is throughout God's Word. Active Christians and ministers must take up something other than their job, maybe a hobby. I prefer Chess; an excellent game that one could do to help relieve stress and pressure. Well, if hobbies are not the way to go, then exercise and traveling could be the way to go. It does not matter what you do as long as you take many mental, physical, and spiritual stress breaks even while serving. Active Christians are human too and not exempt from the ways of the world nor the stress and pressure that comes with it as well.

GOD'S ROADMAP:

Untreated Stress and Pressure can take a toll on the body. Look at the illustration below

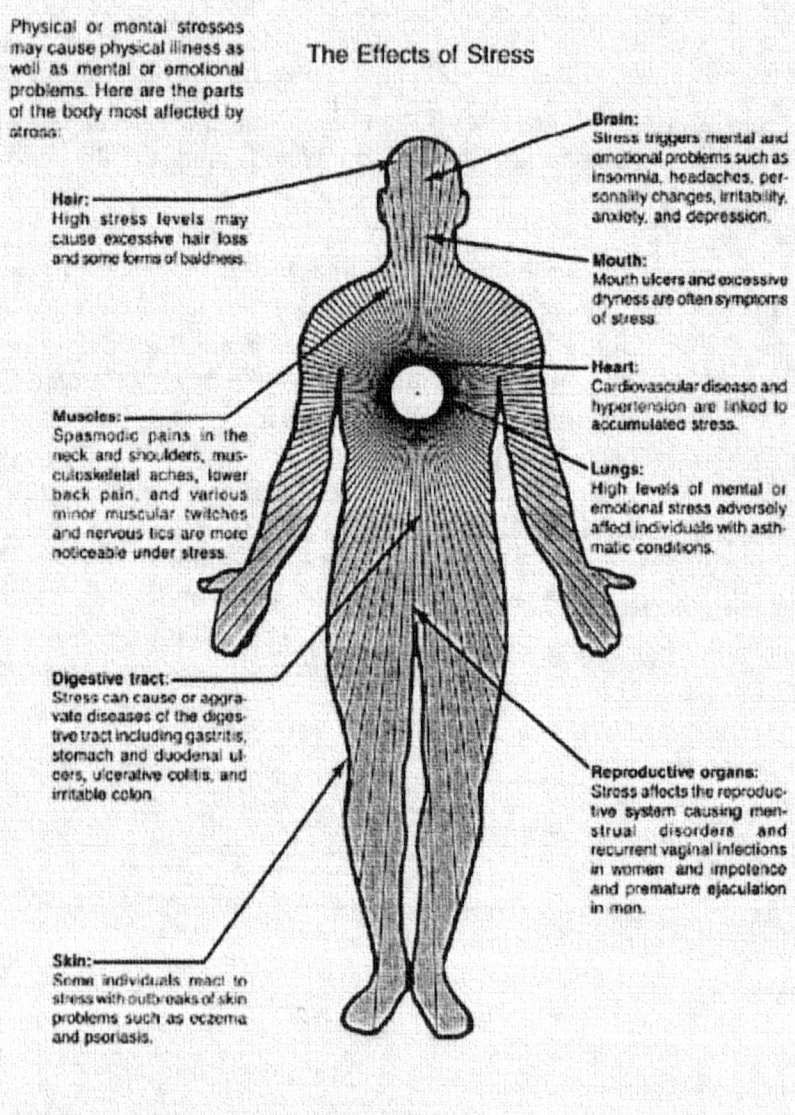

Illustration is from Symptoms' of Stress http://www.stress.org/.

In the survey, five questions specifically addressed one's physical condition as it pertains to their personal experience of stress and pressures. It is evident and conclusive that stress and pressure affects the Active Christians as well as the Average People similarly because we are all human. According to the above diagram, it breaks down how stress and pressure affects our physical bodies.

The only answer to fight stress and pressure is to trust in GOD and live in His ways and not our own. To GOD Be the Glory! GOD covers a multitude of illnesses that we encounter daily and we are not always aware of His blessings of taking them away from us. GOD blesses the whole man: mind, body, and soul.

I leave my favorite Psalm for us all, whenever we are going through stress and pressure; it may seem like we have no way out. Nevertheless, meditate on Psalm 142 by King David. There is rescue and deliverance in God's Word, all we have to do is believe it and grab hold to God's Word. May GOD continue to bless and enrich all of your lives?

Psalm 142: A Contemplation[a] of David. A Prayer when he was in the cave.

¹ I cry out to the LORD with my voice;
    With my voice to the LORD I make my supplication.
² I pour out my complaint before Him;
    I declare before Him my trouble.
³ When my spirit was overwhelmed within me,
    Then You knew my path.
    In the way in which I walk
    They have secretly set a snare for me.
⁴ Look on *my* right hand and see,
    For *there is* no one who acknowledges me;
    Refuge has failed me;
    No one cares for my soul.
⁵ I cried out to You, O LORD:
    I said, "You *are* my refuge,
    My portion in the land of the living.

[6] Attend to my cry,
    For I am brought very low;
    Deliver me from my persecutors,
    For they are stronger than I.
[7] Bring my soul out of prison,
    That I may praise Your name;
    The righteous shall surround me,
    For You shall deal bountifully with me."

This was David crying for help. He was experiencing stress and pressure in every aspect of his life: mentally, physically, and spiritually. His petition was for GOD to deliver him in every way. I personally felt every bit of David's complaint before the LORD. I too was in similar position, and JESUS delivered me just as he did with King David, and GOD is waiting to do the same for us. We just only have to ask JESUS to come into our life and save us, a sinner. Believe JESUS is the SON of GOD who died for our sins at Calvary and Rose for our Justification on the third daily bodily alive.

References

Adams, Jay E. (1970). Competent To Counsel. Zondervan, Grand Rapids, Michigan

Bandura, A. (1992) Exercise of Personal Agency through the Self-Efficacy Mechanisms. In R. Schwarzer (Ed.), Self-Efficacy: Thought Control of Action. Washington, DC

Bandura, A. (1994). Self-Efficacy. In V. S. Ramachaudran (Ed.), Encyclopedia of Human Behavior, 4. New York: Academic Press, pp. 71-81.

Brown, Elizabeth B. (2006). Living Successfully with Screwed-Up People. Baker Publishing Group. Grand Rapids, Michigan

Christian Counseling (2004 ed.). International Institute of Faith Based Counseling. Life Training Institute, Inc. Texas.

Crouch, Van. (1998). Take It Back! Albury Publishing Tulsa, Oklahoma

D'Zurilla, T. J., & Sheedy, C. F. (1991). Relation between social problem-solving among college suicide ideators and non-Ideators. College Student Journal, 30, 377-384.

"Dealing with Stress." [Online] Available at
http://www.teenmailbiblestudy.org/2007/03/dealing_with_stress.html
March 9, 2007 by Carl Hanson

Diehm, William J. Ph.D. (1994). 6 Sure ways To Solve Any Problem:
Refer-   What Broadman & Holman Publishers. New York.

Evangelical Training Association (2002 ed.). Biblical Beliefs. Zondervan Publishing House.

Hirsch, J. K., & Ellis, J. B. (1996). Differences in life stress and reasons
for living among college suicide ideators and non-Ideators. College
Student Journal, 30, 377-384.

Jakes, T.D. (1997). So You Call Yourself A Man? Bethany House
Minneapolis., Minn.

Kiffer, Jerome F. MA., Department of Health Psychology and Applied
Psychophysiology, The Cleveland Clinic Foundation

Misra, R., McKean, M., West, S., & Russo, T. (2000). Academic
Stress of College Students: Comparison of Student and Faculty Perceptions. College Student Journal, June 2000.

Omartian, Stormie. (2001). The Power of a Praying Husband. Harvest
House Publishers. Eugene Oregon.

Ross, S. E., Niebling, B. C., & Heckert, T. M. (1999). Sources of Stress Among College Students. College Student Journal, June 1999.

Stafford, Wess Ph.D. (2007). Too Small to Ignore: Why the Least of These Matters Most. Water Brook Press. New York.

"Stress in the Clergy: Today's Ministers Expected to Do Too Much." [Online] Available at http://www.mlive.com/living/grand rapids/index.ssf/2010/11/stress_in_the_clergy_todays_mi.html November 13, 2010

"Stress Management Exercises." [Online] Available at http://www.innerhealthstudio.com/stress-management-exercises.html October 14, 2010. "Symptoms of Stress." [Online] Available at www.innerhealthstudio.com/symptoms-of-stress.html. November 6, 2010

The King James Bible, Authorized King James Version. (1985 ed.). Nashville, TN. Thomas Nelson Publishers.

Vander, A. J., Sherwood, J. H., & Luciano D. S. Human Physiology: From Cells to System. 4th Edition by McGraw Hill, 2001